Ten
about

Candlestick Press

Published by:
Candlestick Press,
Diversity House, 72 Nottingham Road, Arnold, Nottingham NG5 6LF, UK
https://www.candlestickpress.co.uk/

Design and typesetting by Craig Twigg

Printed by Bayliss Printing Company Ltd of Worksop, UK

First published 2011
Reprinted 2011, 2012, 2014, 2015, 2016

Second edition, revised 2019
Reprinted 2021, 2023, 2024 (twice)

Third edition, revised 2025

ISBN 978 1 913627 72 0

Acknowledgements

The poems in this pamphlet are reprinted from the following books, all by permission of the publishers listed unless stated otherwise. Every effort has been made to trace the copyright holders of the poems published in this book. The editor and publisher apologise if any material has been included without permission, or without the appropriate acknowledgement, and would be glad to be told of anyone who has not been consulted.

Thanks are due to all the copyright holders cited below for their kind permission.

Laurie Bolger, *Lady* (Nine Arches Press, 2025). Maura Dooley, *Sound Barrier: Poems 1982-2002* (Bloodaxe Books, 2002) www.bloodaxebooks.com. Jonathan Edwards, *My Family and Other Superheroes* (Seren Books, 2014) by kind permission of the author. Joanna Ingham, *Poetry Wales Spring 2021 Volume 56 Number 3*., by kind permission of the author. Jackie Kay, *Darling: New & Selected Poems* (Bloodaxe Books, 2007) www.bloodaxebooks.com. Roy McFarlane, *Living by Troubled Waters* (Nine Arches Press, 2022). Carmina Masoliver, *The Northern Gravy Anthology of Poetry*, ed. Ralph Dartford (Northern Gravy, 2025) by kind permission of the author. Caleb Parkin, *This Fruiting Body* (Nine Arches Press, 2021). John Siddique, first published in *The Prize* (Rialto 2005) by kind permission of the author.

All permissions cleared courtesy of Dr Suzanne Fairless-Aitken
c/o Swift Permissions swiftpermissions@gmail.com.

Where poets are no longer living, their dates are given.

Contents **Page**

To my mother, aged 10

You will not always be the fat girl,
parents behind the counter
at the corner shop, jars full of sweets.
There will be friends. There will be
dance classes and *Country Roads*,
your husband in his orange shirt,
that brocade tie. There will be daughters.
There will be an accident, but it will not
take everything all at once. You will learn
to see in colour again, a blackbird's beak
yolk yellow. You will not always
feel stupid. There will be children
who listen in classrooms, who stroke
your support tights. There will be
operations, veins stripped from your legs,
scars and new knees. But you will walk
fast, pumping your arms. There will be
last breaths, and you will hear them,
but there will be parties too, gardens
you cut into shape. You will not always
be alone. You will not be the hairdresser
your father wants you to be. You will
find your own path, teach a boy to speak
instead of growl, stitch and felt and make.
Don't cry. You will come to understand
the bullies. Anyway, I'm here, waiting
for you to push me into being.

Joanna Ingham

The Voice in which my Mother Read to Me

isn't her good morning, good afternoon, good night voice,
her karaoke as she dusts, make furniture polite voice,
her saved for neighbours' babies and cooing our dog's name voice.

It isn't her best china, not too forward, not too shy voice,
or her dinner's ready, your room looks like a sty voice,
or her whisper in my ear as she adjusts my tie voice.

It's not her roll in, Friday night, *Lucy in the Sky* voice,
her Sunday morning, smartest frock, twinkle-in-the-eye voice,
that passing gossip of the vicar with the Communion wine voice.

It's not her 'Gateau – no, ice cream – no... I can't make
the choice' voice.
It's not her decades late, fourth change, 'Is this skirt
smart enough?' voice.
It's not her caught me with the girl from number twenty-one voice.

That voice which she reserved for twelve-foot grannies,
Deep South hobos,
that sleepy, secret staircase, selfish giants, Lilliput voice.
That tripping over, 'Boy, why is your house so full of books?' voice.

Jonathan Edwards

Mum

Your telephone voice and your telling me
to speak properly amuses me,
as you say in your drama teacher way,
I still need to have my bath!

Born to Yorkshire working class
parents of the parish, though you are
so far away from that now, the sound
of granddad's trumpet is still
music to your ears.

And these years are your adventure,
though sometimes you're not so sure,
look at your first class degree
you got after being pregnant with me,
look at the man you're still with, my dad,
and the battles you still live through.

You need to look at the play
you said you wanted to throw away
but always turns out amazing on the day,
look at your heart,
look at its beating with love,
look at all the things you do,
look at, look at – would you just look at *you*.

Carmina Masoliver

I try my absolute best

I give my kids pure apple juice
(no sugar less acid than orange)
buy my baby soya milk formula
now she's off the breast
(non dairy, no cholesterol, good
for their little hearts – apparently
their arteries can harden before five
even). Water from the purifier.
Perrier if I'm feeling flush
(they can always pretend it's lemonade).
Carob-coated date bars. Cherry or banana.
And there's a shop down the street
that is selling organic vegetables
(no sprays, no chemicals).
Only to find the bloody English apples
are being sprayed with Alar and are
carcinogenic; the soya beans are cooked
in aluminium pots which gives off deposits
in the brain; the cartridge in the purifier
collects things (like knickers if they're not changed).
Perrier's got Benzene in it which gives rats
cancer. Though I personally don't know any rat
that drinks Perrier, do you? And them
so-called Health Food Bars contain more sugar
than the average Mars Bar. What's the use
in calling anything organic when
the bloody soil's chock-a-block with lead?

I try my absolute best,
drink decaff coffee to pipe me down
instead of hype me up only to find
out from my eldest daughter
that what they put the beans through
is worse for you than an ordinary Nescafé.

I’m back on Valium.
My kids are stuffing Monster Munch
and Mars Bars down them.
My youngest son even ate a hamburger yesterday.
It’s driving me crazy.
I says it’s your pocket money,
Do what you want with it.

Jackie Kay

Mothers of Love

I can affirm, that the affections between the mothers and even spurious offspring are very powerful as well as permanent…

– Edward Kamau Brathwaite, *Folk Culture of the Slaves in Jamaica*

Mothers, wherever they saw us,
always greeted us in love.

Mother Hill folded it
with portions of healings

in the name of Jesus.
Mother Rowe cooked it

in Dutch pots of laughter.
Mother Russell golden brown,

shimmered in the beauty of it.
Mother Dawkins' table

overflowed with it
and toto and rum cake too.

Mother Henry planted it
in pots and tended to them.

Mother Taylor sung and danced
under a moon touched by it.

Mother Caine spoke
in the softness of aloe vera.

Mother Stanley spared
not the rod. Mother Douglas

sent bags of it. Mother Ruby
soaked dried fruits in it

for Christmas cakes. Mother Brown
prayed for rain and rivers of it.

Mother Miller sent it
by air mail from Jamaica.

Mother Foulkes mixed it
with stories and proverbs.

Mother Edwards picked it up
at the market and passed it on

to Mother Campbell who shared
without hesitation and Mother Hill

can be found late at night
folding more for a new day.

Roy McFarlane

Roots

Mum's grown out her grey
less foil   less dye

I've stopped wiping colour
          corrector all over my face
                    chalky mint green

she says isn't it funny how we dress
          sloppy now   just casual
                    whatever we want –

I want to say I think we are so beautiful
                              sat outside the coffee shop
                                        being honest in the cold.

Laurie Bolger

Cheap Moisturiser

I worry every time I see her it may be
the last time. My mother is 74 this year,
that age when, if she doesn't answer
the phone, my stomach backspins.

Today I massaged her hands with moisturiser,
with drops of lavender mixed in it. Her arthritis
is really bad in her left hand. The thumb
closing over the palm. Her middle finger
thick ropey gristle beneath tissue transparent skin.

This is the first time we've done such a thing.
Mother objects at first, but begins to enjoy
my fingers pressing her fingers; the muscle-root
in her forearm, the small marbles that roll
across the muscle.

Often these days we dance to Abba or Queen,
quick two minute waltzes on her green cat-haired
rug that's always crooked. She's not been touched
much in her life. I die if a day goes by without a love.

She never hugged us once we'd stopped being small.
My sisters and I are knotty trees in
mum's garden. Now I try to feed and care
for her with lavender oil and hands, hoping
some of the love I taught myself will soak
into her fingers, and backflow into
her body, through the fibres she has grown
over her untouched desire.

John Siddique

If the Earth is My Mother

then the Earth yodels in carparks and stairwells. She tells endless tales
over morning tea leaves, while she gossips in customary understories.

If the Earth is my mother, she's a composer of gin and free-poured song,
a knitter of waste-wool, a forager of material, a seamstress of the surplus.

The Earth is a feeder: baker of suet islands on bubbling oceans of stew –
cook for several hundred million imagined diners. A wearer of outlandish wigs.

When Earth doesn't call, that's the worry; she gives too much away in her silences.
If the Earth is my mother, she's had IVs and pipelines fitted, right to her heart.

Earth has evolved, changed landscape. She finds it hard to rest,
even after a long and chemical winter, a malignant aftermath.

She knows her own and her neighbours' maladies, her own and others' offspring.
Earth will mother you all, if you'll let her (or even if you won't). If the Earth is

any kind of step-, -in-law, drag, foster, second, adoptive, convoluted, maddening mother
to you, then it's time you called her – right now – so she can let you know   it's serious.

Caleb Parkin

Piano

Softly, in the dusk, a woman is singing to me;
Taking me back down the vista of years, till I see
A child sitting under the piano, in the boom of the tingling
  strings
And pressing the small, poised feet of a mother who smiles
  as she sings.

In spite of myself, the insidious mastery of song
Betrays me back, till the heart of me weeps to belong
To the old Sunday evenings at home, with winter outside
And hymns in the cosy parlour, the tinkling piano our
  guide.

So now it is vain for the singer to burst into clamour
With the great black piano appassionato. The glamour
Of childish days is upon me, my manhood is cast
Down in the flood of remembrance, I weep like a child for
  the past.

DH Lawrence (1885 – 1930)

Mirror

In my mother's house
is the friendly mirror,
the only glass in which I look
and think I see myself,
think, yes, that's what
I think I'm like,
that's who I am. The only
glass in which I look and smile.

Just as this baby smiles
at the baby who always
smiles at her, the one in
her mother's arms, the mother
who looks like me, who
smiles at herself in her
mother's mirror, the friendly
mirror in her mother's house.

But if I move to one side
we vanish, the woman I thought
was me, the baby making friends
with herself, we move to one side
and the mirror holds no future, no past,
in its liquid frame, only the corner
of an open window, a bee visiting
the ready flowers of summer.

Maura Dooley